What do I

I started my educational career ma   atics Teacher in a couple of extremely diffic   ade up of not the most discerning of the educational system.

Within a very short period of time and whilst on a very steep learning curve and with a great deal of support from a superb staff team, I very quickly found my vocation. This, surprisingly, was not just teaching mathematics but teaching mathematics to some of the most disaffected and challenging students at the secondary school. It became apparent that I had a particular set of skills that enabled me to get through and relate to the students who didn't want to, or in fact couldn't, conform.

My timetable started to become littered with the Set 5 Red (Red for danger!!) and they would normally give them to me on a Friday afternoon (Graveyard shift).

I actually enjoyed the challenge and so when a job was advertised at a FE college that was closer to my residence came up, teaching the unteachable, the students who had been excluded from local secondary schools I was first in line. During this time at the college I was privileged to not only teach the excludees but also taught all ages spanning up to 80 year olds who were writing their will and testament in one of my ICT classes. Whilst employed at the college I also spent time teaching soldiers in the local barracks and prisoners at the near-by prison.

After a period of time the Pupil Referral Unit in the area were sending young people to me and one day I was visited by the Headteacher who asked if I would join the team, which I willingly accepted.

I then spent the majority of my educational career working with and for the PRU system which allowed me to dip my toe into the KS2 end of the education spectrum, completing time as a Behaviour Advisory Teacher and elevating myself through the ranks up to the heady heights of the senior leadership team and running my own PRU before moving onto head up a residential learning environment.

I have been lucky enough to deliver training around Restorative Practice, Behaviour Management and Positive Mindsets to any number of whole school staff, conferences and teacher training institutions.

I wanted to write this book as I am aware of a huge number of books on the market that go in depth into the wheres and hows of behaviour and I wanted a no nonsense read which was down to earth to the point and could be referenced quickly and easily. Yes the psychology of every individual you teach is highly important and should be taken into consideration, however, there is a need to sometimes have a tool box ready for when the proverbial hits the fan in front of your very eyes and which you have to be able to deal with.

I hope you enjoy it and find it useful and good luck with whatever stage of your educational career you are at.

Chapter One:
Relationships

Relationships are key and the most important factor in any walk of life, whether it is in business, personal or educational settings. If you cannot build strong positive relationships with people you are going to struggle.

Being able to build and rebuild relationships with your clientele is extremely important and should not be under estimated.

TASK:
Take a minute just to think about how you build strong, positive relationships with the students you teach on a daily basis.

I am guessing/hoping that you immediately started thinking about the conversations that you may have had with students, the time spent with different groups of children etc.

Some of the things I would recommend are as follows:

Get to know your clientele as much as possible.

This includes things like showing an interest in their hobbies/likes/dislikes. I once had an extremely difficult individual in one of my classes so I went out of my way to find out what his particular interests were. Much to my disappointment he was a Manchester United fan, this is not because I dislike Manchester United but more to do with my utter hatred of the game of football. I would, however, not let my feelings towards football get in the way of trying to build a professional relationship with this student. It didn't take much on my part to listen to the news on the way into work or catch the scores the night before so that when I saw the student I could make a throwaway comment regarding whether his team had won or lost with a facial expression thrown in for good measure to open up a conversation. After a week or two of this I found myself enjoying teaching the class a whole lot more as the difficult individual was now 'onside', no pun intended, but also as a result because he felt more comfortable with me he was open to actually learning whilst in my classroom.
I would also suggest finding out who your students live with. Gone are the days that most students live with Mum and Dad. More likely these days they either live between the two or occasionally with Carers, Uncles, Aunties, Grandparents or any number of other extended family members.

Also do they have siblings living at the same address. This seems like an almost impossible task, particularly if you teach in the secondary sector where you may have 150 students cross your classroom threshold on a daily basis. I can't stress, however, how important this could be. A colleague of mine once made the mistake of not doing his homework with a student in his cohort. The student had been acting out for sometime in one of their lessons and after warning on a number of occasions was heard to utter the phrase 'If you continue to behave like this I will phone your Mum'. Little did my colleague know the students mother had died recently. You can imagine the nuclear explosion that followed! This also damaged my colleagues relationship with the student indefinitely and also damaged the relationship my colleague had with that entire group of students which took a significant period of time to rebuild. Know the triggers or antecedents of their behaviour.

Correct names are vital.

In a previous incarnation as a Behaviour Advisory Teacher I would often be asked to observe groups of students or particular students who had been identified by staff as being 'difficult'. As a result of this I would often sit myself at the back of classrooms and make notes. I cannot tell you how many students would complain to me about the teacher getting their name wrong, this would often follow a very keen student putting their hand in the air appropriately to answer the question that had just been posed only to be pointed at an called the incorrect name. The body language of the student immediately changed and would often indicate that they felt worthless, this would also lessen the chance of the student repeating the embarrassing ordeal of placing their hand in the air to answer another question.

Make sure Nicknames are appropriate and wanted.

I learnt this valuable lesson following another colleagues mistake. Every time I meet a new student I always ask 'What do you like to be called?' This may sound like a ridiculous question but it has kept me out of trouble on a number of occasions. The colleague I refer to above had a new student join one of his groups and the young lady was introduced to him, by the Head of Year, as Charlie. The young girl in question was very well behaved and although she quickly made a number of friends and seemed to get along with the majority of the staff, my colleague was struggling to engage her in his lessons and the student would also not engage in conversation with him. On a number of occasions he would ask if she was alright, whether she found the work difficult, whether she didn't get on with other students in the class but he was met with a blank look and normally a shrug of the shoulders. After a number of weeks he decided to have another attempt to get to the bottom of what was going wrong. Finally he said 'Is it me? Am I doing something to upset you? At this point the conversation turned to the fact that her name was actually Charlotte and she hated being called Charlie. She hadn't felt comfortable or confident enough to let him know beforehand. Following this conversation the relationship got stronger and Charlotte engaged far more and therefore increased her rate of progress in my colleagues subject.

Concentrate on the 'difficult' students.

A lot of teachers feel they have excellent relationships with students but fail to realise that the students they have the strong relationships with are the well behaved, engaged, keen to learn students. No offence, but these are the easy relationships to develop and maintain. The students who complete all their homework on time, have often got their hands in the air keen to answer questions, complete all the tasks set in class and who happily will stay behind to ask further questions are the students who take very little effort, on your part, to build rapport with. It is the student who sits at the back of the classroom making little or no effort in lessons whilst not engaging are the ones you need to spend a little more energy on. The association you have with these challenging students can make your life in the classroom a great deal easier. Build positive, professional connections with these individuals by giving yourself some time to get to know them and I am sure you will notice a significant difference.

Extra-curricular activities.

In my opinion the majority of students do not see teachers as 'human beings'. This may sound strange, nonetheless, I truly believe that they see us as 'Authority Figures', 'Educational Robots', 'the enemy', etc. Some of the students I have taught in the past have been truly surprised to see me with my family out and about enjoying myself during weekends and holidays as they do not think about teachers having lives outside school. Extra-curricular activities allow students to see you outside of your natural environment and with some of your barriers down. I am always amazed at the reactions of students when they see staff in casual clothes and tracksuits. Extra-curricular activities give you as the staff member opportunity to show your human side which in turn breaks down barriers between staff and student.

Acknowledge students wherever they maybe.

In my role as a Behaviour Advisory Teacher I was in a privileged position to spend time in a large number of educational establishments. Whilst in these schools / colleges / academies I would often spend some time wandering the corridors observing what was happening outside the classroom environment as much as what was happening inside the classes. By spending this quality time on the corridors I was able to assess what the culture and ethos of the establishment was. Observing:
- How many students were stood outside the classrooms?
- Were there a number of students seemingly wandering the corridors aimlessly?
- Were these students being challenged?
- What was the standard of uniform being worn? Shirts out, trainers on, tie being worn correctly?

The list goes on.

The biggest observation I would make amongst all these institutions is the interaction between staff and students on the corridors and, to be more specific, the lack of it. On the rare occasions that students were acknowledged the majority of these interactions were very accusatory. Staff would often focus solely on the negatives.

Then there were what I would refer to as the 'blinkered teachers'. These are the staff who would prowl the corridors without seeing or hearing any student, focussed on the brew that is waiting for them in the staff room, rather than everything else that is happening around them. Students can readily identify these staff by name and due to this behaviour they become victims of their own passiveness. Students very quickly recognise that these staff will not effectively challenge or even acknowledge the students presence, this allows for the students to act, behave in any fashion they desire in the knowledge that the staff member will not challenge.

Acknowledge students on the corridor in a positive way notice if they have had a haircut, compliment them on being smart and if they are wearing the correct footwear, make mention of appropriate behaviour you witness and good manners. Simply paying attention on the corridors will not only improve your relationships with students but will also create a reputation for being one of the good/nice guys. This will also give you opportunities to tackle behaviour and be proactive building your reputation for being able to deal with behaviour appropriately.

Positive communication with home (Parents / Carers).

The final suggestion I am going to make is to make positive contact with home as often as possible. As teachers we are very good at contacting home as and when students behave badly, we tend not to be as good at contacting home when students have behaved well. This is imperative if relationships are to be built and maintained with students. Some of the students, that display challenging behaviour, may have never had positive feedback sent home. As a result of the positive feedback you give to parents/carers the student very well may benefit from rewards on arrival home. This not only strengthens the bond between parents and student but also between child and staff, and staff and parents.
I call this the 'GOLDEN TRIANGLE'.

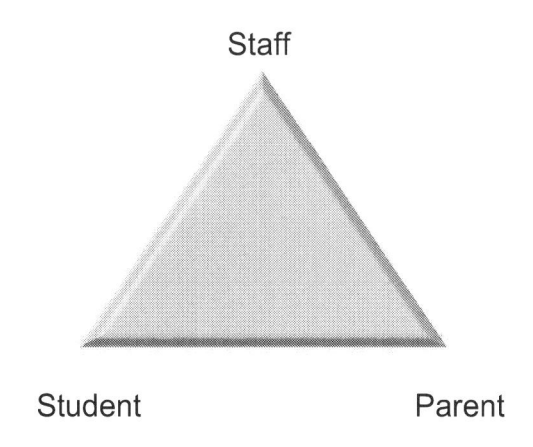

Staff

Student   Parent

If all three components of the Golden Triangle are working in unison you are able to move mountains. The student will often try to break the Triangle by driving a wedge between staff and parents, it is important at these junctures that contact is made and decisions/issues are discussed as soon as possible in order to rebuild and strengthen the Triangle.

All the above comes with a caveat, although you are hoping to build and maintain positive, professional relationships with the students this has to be built on a foundation of respect. This is extremely important as you do not and cannot be the students 'mate', 'friend'. All too often I have seen, particularly, young teachers feel that they are 'down with the kids' and pay the price later in the year. If you have any doubt about how this can go wrong I urge you to watch the comedy sketch by Jack Dee, link below, which highlights this issue.

https://www.youtube.com/watch?v=1c5Z9jpA0nw

Respect is key and fortunately or unfortunately, depending on your point of view, gone are the days where respect is a given. When I was growing up I was always told to respect my elders. These days children do not have this drilled into them and instead are very much given permission to question elders and see them as equals. If done in the correct way this is an extremely good quality to have. The challenging students amongst the crowd will often abuse this right and question decisions in an inappropriate way. It is for this reason that we have to teach that respect is earned and not a given. We have to earn their respect as much as they have to earn ours. How do we earn respect? Treating people in a firm but fair way, explaining why decisions are being made and being consistent.

TASK:
Take a minute just to think about how you build strong, positive relationships with Parents / Carers.

Most teachers find this question more difficult to answer, but I feel this is just as important a question to answer as outlined previously when I was describing the 'GOLDEN TRIANGLE'.

The key to these relationships is once again communication. Positive communication with Parents / Carers is imperative. There have been numerous incidences of students who have arrived at the PRU I was managing with parents who would not pick up the phone to us simply due to the fact that the only communication from education previously has been to give them negative information about their child. It is for this reason that I purchased a 'Pay as you go' mobile phone for the PRU which may sound strange. The sole purpose of this phone was to be used for the first phone call to parents after a new student had arrived with us. The rule was that this phone could *not* be used for negative feedback, positive feedback on behaviour or academic achievements only. This was to manipulate parents into picking up an unknown number, rather than the school phone number, and giving them some positive news about their child. This worked exceptionally well and the parents often, not only answered their phone but also reacted with surprise and glee at the fact their child was getting positive, nice things said about them. This is the first step to the 'GOLDEN TRIANGLE'. Once this process had been started with the phone call I encouraged all staff to communicate with parents regularly. These days there are a number of options such as group texts, website, blog, email etc. which makes communication so much easier and quicker than previous. During these communications I would also promote that staff would invite parents in to the centre in order to view their child's work and discuss progress. Parents evenings are so formal, by inviting them in and giving them time makes the parents feel special and increases the bond between staff and parents.

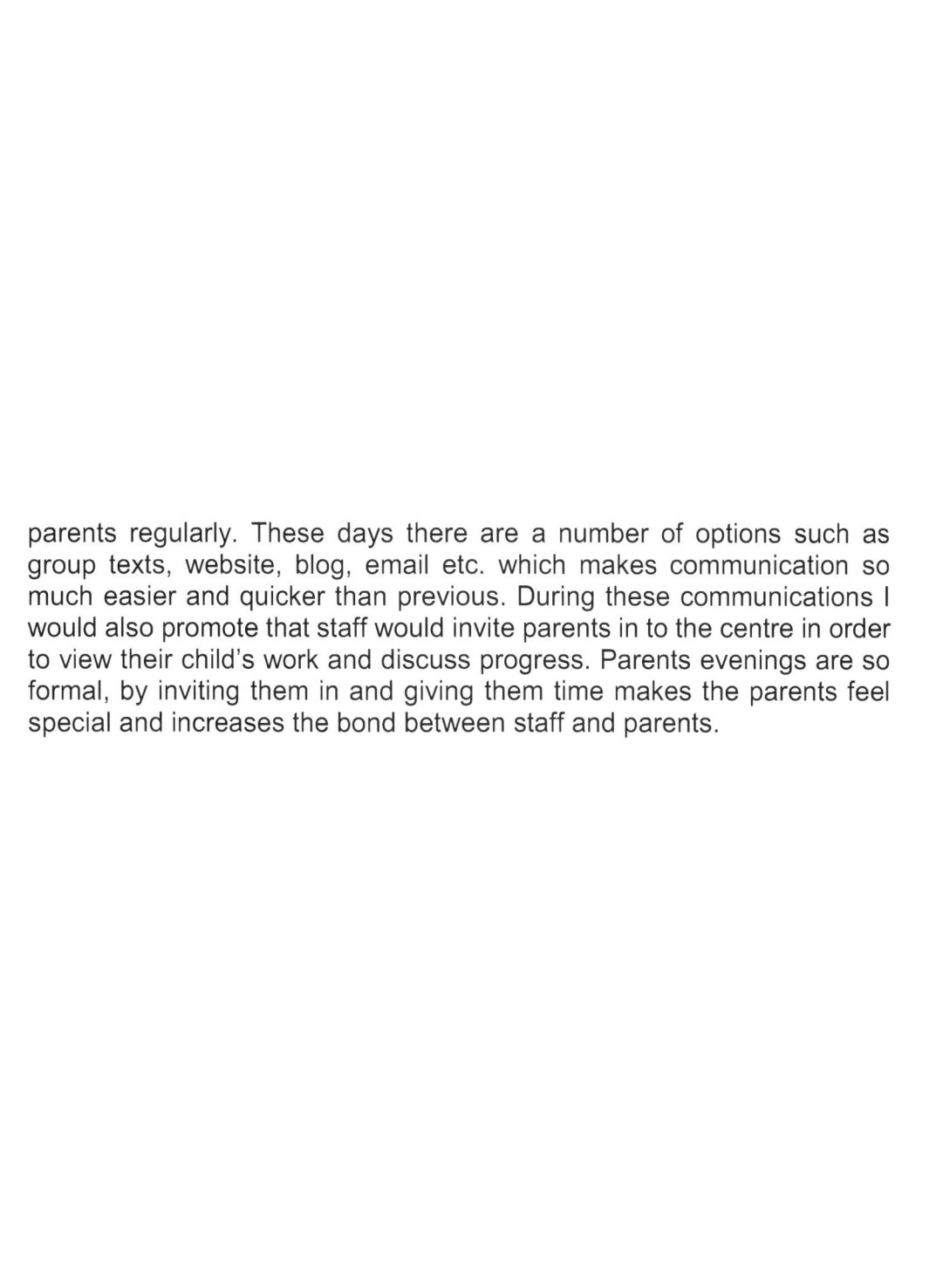

Chapter Two:
POSITIVITY

Before I get started on positivity in the classroom I first feel it necessary to climb onto my soapbox.

I need you to think about the worst behaved student you have in your classes. Now it is my belief that no-one is born bad and also that the vast majority of behaviour is a choice (obviously there are some medical conditions where behaviour is a symptom of the diagnosis). The problem is that some students make the wrong choices based on a distorted way they look at life.

Some students within your groups will have ridiculously chaotic lifestyles and as a result they have had to adapt in order to survive. These same students may be operating with 'learnt behaviours' which have had a positive outcome for them in the past.
The students who display the most challenging behaviour are often the students who have the most unstable and chaotic home lives.
Just for a moment put yourself in their shoes:
They may come from homes that are on the breadline, where they are struggling to find the next meal or on the verge of being evicted. Domestic abusive / violent backgrounds where they are living constantly on the edge and have seen and heard things that they cannot 'unsee' or 'unhear'.

These students arrive in school with a higher base level of stress, anxiety and therefore it doesn't take much to tip them over the edge. Imagine how far down the priority list Homework, Punctuality, Attendance, Algebra and correct Grammar is if you do not know whether you will have a roof over your head on arrival home or whether there will be anything to eat or even dreading going home for fear of getting a beating or seeing your loved ones receiving an unprovoked attack. For some of these individuals a detention keeps them away from the abusive, stressful environment and therefore they could be looking for an excuse not to go home.
School will probably be the most stable, safe environment they experience.

Even for the children in fairly stable backgrounds or adults for that matter the world offers up so much negativity that it has become the norm.

Think about a typical evening in the majority of households. A diet of Soap Operas which seem to me to be increasingly depressing in content, followed by the News, which is always a bundle of laughs!! Any teenagers who are still watching TV would probably at this point disappear into a dark bedroom to shoot zombies on a computer game whilst insulting Americans on their headset until daft o'clock in the morning.
NEGATIVE, NEGATIVE, NEGATIVE!!
Talking briefly about Soap Operas as mentioned above here is a task I often set participants on the courses I deliver.

TASK:
Try and name a soap opera character that has done well for themselves and been extremely successful, legally (without doing any dodgy deals with undesirables or stealing / breaking the law etc.) and not have something horrendous happen to them soon after they have become successful.

I have issued this task to hundreds of participants and as yet no-one has been able to come up with an individual that is portrayed on any of the soap operas. These are the role-models we are putting in front of our young people. These role-models are force feeding the young minds we work with that in order to be successful you have to:
- Be dodgy
- Break the law
- Be greedy and thoughtless
- Be nasty to, and use other people

Once you have become successful by any means necessary, at that point something horrible will befall you.
Basically the message we are giving our youngsters is:

Success is bad!!

It is for the reasons, that I have outlined above, that I truly believe that as teachers within an educational establishment, we have to make the hours that the students attend, the most positive environment they may experience.

The Law of Attraction states that Positivity attracts Positivity and vice versa Negativity attracts Negativity. If you surround yourself with negative environments and negative thoughts then you will focus on the issues around them and create a self-fulfilling prophecy which will be woe and misery, on the flip side those who can see and focus on the positive aspects of their life will undoubtedly see more opportunities and solutions to overcome the issues. I often ask people how their day has been, I am regularly told they have had a bad day. When I focus them into what has actually been the problem(s) the actual time they have spent dealing with such issues has been minimal, normally lasting no more than half an hour at most. If you put this in perspective this dictates that out of a normal working day of eight hours, seven and a half of these hours were positive therefore over 90% of their working day was positive they just choose to focus on the negative aspects.

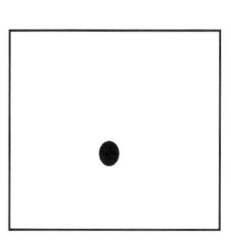

When shown the diagram above and asked what do you see, most people will focus on the black dot in the middle of the white square. The black dot represents the negative and therefore we need to be focussing on the amount of white square which surrounds the dot which represents the positive.

Which element of the above did you focus on?

It is our role not only to educate students in our chosen subjects but also to teach them about aspirations, inspire and motivate them to achieve goals and be the best they can be. Teach them that hard work, determination and practice drives them towards being successful in whatever they choose to be or do.

How do we do this?

Be a role model.

We as professional adults need to role model the behaviour we expect from the students who watch our every move intently. This dictates that we have high expectations of ourselves, not just our students. We need to have an excellent attendance record and be consistent and fair when dealing with issues. We should be demonstrating effective communication skills at all times and how to manage our state in times of stress. As mentioned in the previous chapter we need to earn respect and not just expect it.

There are three types of staff in any school which can be defined by the following words.
- PASSIVE
- ASSERTIVE
- HOSTILE

I am sure that given these descriptive words you would be able to identify colleagues that personify them. Obviously, we should all be striving to be Assertive teachers rather than falling into one of the other two categories.

Make a good first impression every lesson.

As a teacher it is you who creates the ethos in your classroom and sets the tone. This is created even before the student crosses the threshold of your classroom and takes his or her seat. By welcoming the students at the door with a friendly tone and being organised enough to have some starter activities for them on arrival you are creating an atmosphere of confidence in yourself and the students while also establishing a safe environment.

Meeting and greeting students at the door is, in my view, imperative. I found, over the years, that most issues and behaviour within the classroom is as a direct result of things that have happened outside of the classroom. Just a few examples of this maybe:
- Break times
- Lunch times
- Transition of sessions
- Social Media

By meeting and greeting the students at the door it gives you the perfect opportunity to quickly assess the facial expressions and body language of the arriving students and make a judgement call as to whether they are in the correct frame of mind for learning. It is at this point you can attempt to challenge and deal with these situations before the individuals enter the classroom. This also makes it very clear to students that on entering your class they are entering a learning zone.

Later in this book I will discuss a strategy known as FUFT. This stands for Follow Up and Follow Through. Part of this strategy prescribes that if you have had any issues with a challenging student and their behaviour, that before you teach them again you meet with them restoratively and address any issues. This allows a clean slate to be in place for the next timetabled session.

Be upbeat and Smile.

This is just as important outside the classroom as it is in. As mentioned earlier, positivity attracts positivity, and therefore if you walk around hunched over with a face on you like a wet weekend, looking like you have the weight of the world on your shoulders a number of things will transpire. First your outlook on life will be focussed on the negative and therefore more negativity will befall you. Second people will avoid you, many individuals will shy away from you as they do not want to be dragged down with you. You may be lucky enough to have a very close friend who may ask you what is wrong, guaranteed they will be wishing they hadn't 5 minutes later OR they will be feeding your negativity by joining in with you doubling up in the misery stakes. The third thing that will happen is you will miss all sorts of things that are going on around you which makes you one of the blinkered teachers I discussed previously.

I have the antidote. Smile!! Wide eyes and head held high. This may be difficult at times, however, it is important you try your level best to achieve the slightly manic expression. If you are into sports you would call it 'Your Game Face!' alternatively you may have heard the expression 'Eyes and Teeth!'. Either way, for the most part, it is not the students fault you are generally in a bad mood, it maybe you have had a fall out with your partner, had a flat tyre on the way into work, money troubles etc. it is very rare that it is just the students who are getting you down.

I recall a time during my divorce, each day I would arrive at school with what felt like my world was crumbling around me. As I approached my classroom I had to remind myself that what I was feeling had nothing to do with the young people I was about to teach and that they deserve my best. I used to leave my emotional baggage at the threshold to my room and apply my game face, Smile and welcome the young people into the room where Maths became fun!! By adopting this wide eyed, smiley expression other benefits will become apparent. The students will not be sure what state of mind you are in, as you may look a bit crazy and they may not be used to teachers smiling, this can make them a little bit wary because who knows what a crazy person is capable of. Finally, you will be more aware of your surroundings and will therefore build your reputation of dealing with issues effectively and efficiently as they happen. In essence what I am saying is:

'Look as though you want to be there and that you are enjoying teaching them!'

Young people are very adept at reading facial expressions and body language and they will give you away if you are not careful.

Catch them being good.

As educators we are world experts at catching people who are breaking the rules. I could pride myself on the sixth sense I had which would allow me to identify from where the paper aeroplane had been thrown, who had thrown the offending item and who it was directed at, all as I was facing the white board and giving the next set of instructions to the group. What we need to be more aware of and better at is catching the students who are obeying the rules and praising them as role models. This becomes even more important when you are able to catch your more challenging characters behaving well. This helps rebuild / build relationships and gives you opportunity to contact home and build strong, positive relationships with parents / carers.

Praise and Reward – Be specific.

All human beings enjoy praise. Praising and rewarding someone is one of the biggest motivators and aspiration builders we have at our disposal. Even professional adults need a pat on the back every now and again and you only have to see the reaction of anyone who receives an award or certificate of sorts.
On occasions when I recognised that the staff at one of the centres I managed were unhappy, the first thing I did was to reflect on decisions I had made or the direction I was leading in. To this end I would suspend the normal agenda for the weekly staff meeting and ask them very simple questions:
- 'What is going wrong?'
- 'What am I doing wrong?'

This was sometimes seen as incredibly brave or incredibly stupid!
One of these meetings resonates in my conscious regularly. On asking the second question one of the long-term members of staff stated with confidence 'You're crap at praise!!'. I was absolutely mortified as I made it my daily mission to make the staff at the centre happy and feeling well supported, this included saying thank you regularly. I have to admit that, at first, I thought 'This guy is talking twoddle!!!', however, as I looked at

the other members of staff sat in the circle many of them were nodding their heads in agreement. We went onto discuss this in more detail and what became very evident was that staff were not happy receiving a thank you, but would rather know what they were being thanked for as otherwise the multiple 'thank yous' became meaningless.

The biggest lesson this taught me was that if a group of adult professionals wanted me to be specific regarding praise then what must the teenagers that come through our door want on a daily basis. From that moment on I have always followed a thank you up with the reason for the thank you.

Chapter Three:
Are your lessons worth behaving for?

This is the most important question I ask myself whenever I am planning a lesson. Following planning a lesson, I always work through it as if I am a student. At that point I look at it from a student perspective and wonder how I would receive the lesson. I also bear in mind that my lesson will be in amongst other lessons they will be going to and from during a typical school day. If at this point I feel that I would be bored at any point I change it. If I am going to find the lesson boring, as an intelligent, professional adult with a long attention span then a young person who does not really want to be there is definitely going to get bored, frustrated etc. and a bored, frustrated student is a potential behaviour issue.

The following headings are what I feel are very important to bear in mind when planning any lesson.

Interesting and Engaging:

As outlined above lessons have to grab the students attention from the get go. Failure to do this is will result in issues that you as the teacher will have to deal with. This will take time away from actual teaching and learning for the majority of the students in the classroom. Be proactive and be able to identify the flashpoints in any lesson plan before teaching it. This in effect will give you confidence and a back-up plan for if and when any lesson goes amiss.

Safe:

I am hoping that within your career so far you will have been introduced to Maslows Hierarchy of need. This is extremely important to take into consideration whenever you create an environment within the classroom. In order for students to achieve their true potential they need to have the foundations in place. The most important of all the needs is to feel safe. Creating an environment that students feel safe to fail is imperative. This does not mean that you lower your expectations of the class but does mean you need to nurture a culture where students are confident and resilient enough to ask questions.

'FAIL' – First Attempt In Learning

Develop an ethos that develops resilience and mental toughness through 'Black Box Thinking'. It is my belief that mistakes don't exist unless you choose to make the same mistake over and over again. Mistakes, in my world, are categorised as learning experiences.

Enjoyable and Fun:

I am a big believer that if you enjoy something you want to do more of it. I tried knitting once, as you can imagine I wasn't really good at it and because I did not enjoy it I wasn't motivated to continue. In contrast I wasn't very good at martial arts when I first started, however, because I enjoyed it and was motivated I wanted to do more of it and therefore progressed through the belts at a rapid rate of knots.
My point is that if you enjoy something, you tend to be more successful at it.

Have fun! Teachers are often very serious about their craft, I say 'Have fun and enjoy'. I believe teachers should be entertainers. As teachers we stand in front of an audience delivering performances to participants who have not paid to be there and possibly do not want to be there. If you are not enjoying yourself and having fun then how do you expect your audience to enjoy your lessons. It is your job to create the atmosphere and ethos of your classroom. Do you want that atmosphere to be fun and enjoyable or miserable and dull? You decide!!

Learning Styles:

Hopefully following your training, you will be very aware that individuals learn in different ways. These are described as: Visual, Auditory and Kinaesthetic.

Visual and auditory learners tend to do better within the school environment. As you will know visual learners learn best through watching people complete tasks or reading. By watching the teacher at the front of the class, the Powerpoint presentation or the written word on the whiteboard these learners take in most of the information they need in order to succeed in the task that is set. Auditory learners are possibly the best suited to conventional teaching methods. These learners listen to the spoken word and as teachers often like to hear the sound of their own voice this is key in the way they learn. Conventional teaching is often described as Chalk and Talk, emphasising the fact it is geared towards visual and auditory learners. By all accounts you will probably be hitting these learning styles without even trying, the key to good teaching is to engage all learners and the kinaesthetic learners are often the ones that are the most difficult to engage, unless you teach PE, Sport, Design Technology etc.

After working in a Pupil Referral Unit environment for over a decade and a half I very quickly realised that the overwhelming majority of learners that land in PRUs after not surviving in mainstream educational settings are kinaesthetic learners. Their learning styles are not catered for in the bulk of their lessons. These learners need to be 'doing' and 'active'. Try to think of physical activities that can drive the point home. Get them up and moving about the room experimenting, performing, surveying etc. These are the forgotten children!! Forget about them at your peril!!

Rules and Routines:

During the training I deliver I always ask the teachers participating to raise their hand if they can list **'all'** their classroom rules and routines they deploy in their respective environments. You would be amazed how many of them are unable to list the rules that they themselves have come up with. If the teachers who have made the rules cannot remember all the rules of the classroom how do they expect the students too, particularly when you add the fact that they are moving from one classroom with one set of rules to the next classroom with a slightly different set of rules. It is very important that you have a few rules that you display prominently and stick to religiously. This means that at every opportunity you enforce these rules and routines. The moment you fail to enforce the rules and routines you are on a slippery slope. I am not a betting man, however, I would put money on the fact that the first time you let a rule slip the next time you enforce the rule with another student they will have ammunition to throw back at you in the form of: 'Why are you picking on me, you let them get away with it!!'

Better to be exhausted, satisfied and feeling good at the end of a good day rather than exhausted, depressed and stressed at the end of a bad day!

By choosing teaching as a profession you will always be exhausted at the end of each day, that is a given, however I prefer to be happy.

BE REFLECTIVE!

Chapter Four:
Are you a model?

Before I start this chapter, I need to share what is known as the Social Discipline Window. This is commonly known by anyone who regularly uses Restorative Justice / Practice.

Social Discipline Window:

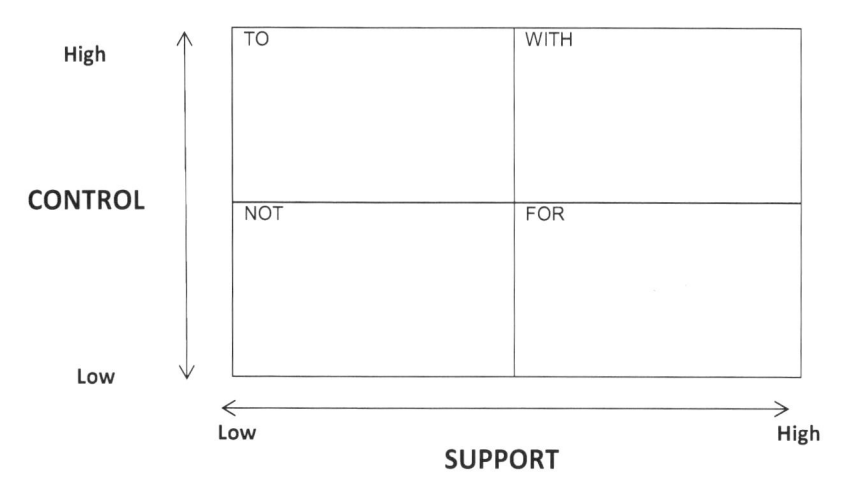

High	TO	WITH
CONTROL	NOT	FOR
Low		
	Low — SUPPORT — High	

What the above diagram illustrates is the different categories that teachers tend to slot into. Of course, it is possible to fit into more than one category depending on what time of the day it is what the weather is like, whether you have had a disagreement with someone before the lesson etc.

TO:
Dictators, Control Freaks, Authoritarians, Tyrants

The 'TO' box contains the staff who display a personality that is high in control and low in support. This would infer that these staff members are the dictators in the classroom. My way or the highway. Punishment and negative consequences are the way forward and if that doesn't work, punish them more. These teachers also tend to fit into the aggressive category.
BASTARDS!

FOR:
Kind, Push over

The 'FOR' box contains the staff who are high in support and low in control. These are your carey, sharey staff who have a stiff neck from all the head tilting in order to communicate their kindness. These are possibly the staff who will do anything for the students and will, at points in the calendar, be taken full advantage of by the students. These teachers also tend to fit into the passive category.
SOFT BASTARDS!

NOT:
Neglectful, Inattentive, Negligent

The 'NOT' box is reserved for staff who are low in control and also low in support. This would suggest the staff, who position themselves in this box, don't do much at all. They are the staff that will do the minimal amount of work to pass muster.
USELESS BASTARDS!

WITH:
Restorative

The 'WITH' box is reserved for the best of us. This is seen as the ideal box to reside in for most of the time. It is also known as the restorative box as this is where you need to be in order to help the young people in your classroom progress quickly, both academically but also socially, as this box will role model the behaviour that you want / need from them. This box can also be described as the assertive box.

Hain Ginnott Quote (1972):

> *I am the decisive element in the classroom*
> *It is my personal approach that creates the climate*
> *It is my daily mood that makes the weather*
> *As a teacher I possess tremendous power to make a childs life miserable or joyous*
> *I can be a tool of torture or an instrument of inspiration*
> *I can humiliate or humour, hurt or heal*

In all situations, it is my response that decides whether a crisis will be escalated or de-escalated, and a child humanized or de-humanized.

Within any of my behaviour management courses, I always include this quote. This sums up the power and influence we have as teachers on a daily / hourly basis.

Role modelling the behaviour you want from the students:

As teachers we could be, for some of our students, the only positive role model in these young peoples' lives. As such we need to not only tell them and instruct them on how to behave but also show them how we need them to conduct themselves. We can only do that if we have the same expectations of ourselves as we do for them.

Assertive staff have these characteristics:
- If we have high expectations for our students we need to have high expectations for ourselves and also transmit these clearly.
- Consistency is extremely important and being firm but fair is key.
- Good attendance and punctuality is also vital. It is what we expect from our students and therefore we should be setting an example. This means getting to your classroom before the students everyday in order to greet them. If a student turns up late to a lesson I have observed teachers give them a real hard time and consequences, however, this same teacher saunters back from the staff room after breaks and expects the students to be waiting in line, quietly awaiting their arrival. 'Double Standards!'
- Effective communication skills are essential. Talk to the students as you expect to be talked to by them. If you are snapping and shouting at the students for the majority of the time, you are stepping into their world and their norm... You will also get a similar response back from said students.
- Linked to this communication they also need to see respectful interactions between other adults and pupils.

The different teaching behaviours that will elicit a response from the young people can be divided into three and their respective traits can be seen below:

STYLE	TEACHING BEHAVIOUR	PUPIL RESPONSE
Passive	- Passive - Inconsistent - Reacts to behaviour - Doesn't plan to manage behaviour - Doesn't have routines - Doesn't communicate boundaries to students - Can be led by students	- Frustration - Tries to manipulate - Escalates situations to explore 'limits' - No respect for teacher - Demonstrates anger - Answers back
Hostile	- Aggressive response to students - Rigid - Authoritarian - Doesn't listen to pupils - Not fair and consistent - Expects bad behaviour and often 'labels' them - Confrontational - Sarcasm	- Fear of making mistakes - Anxious - Low self esteem - Feels victimised - Feelings of hurt - Doesn't take chances in their approach to tasks - Confrontational
Assertive	- Identifies boundaries - States expectations (Academic and Behaviour) - Fair and consistent - Listens to students - Values opinions - Role models behaviour - Humour ('With' not 'At' students) - Praise for effort and achievement	- Understands boundaries - Feels valued - Trust - Passes opinions - Feels safe - Not frightened of making mistakes - More likely to behaviour positively

Which word describes you the best and is it your preferred option?

Chapter Five:
Communication

There are three different types of communication. Most people are aware of Verbal and Non-verbal but very few are aware of the third which is Paraverbal.

Non-Verbal:

Depending on which research you read about non-verbal communication will depend on what percentage of communication is through non-verbal means. However, what all research agrees is that non-verbal communication makes up the majority of how human beings communicate (70% +).
I often describe this in simple terms regarding how we communicate with puppies and babies. Firstly, puppies and babies do not understand the words that they are hearing and therefore from an early age we are learning to pick up on the non-verbal cues we receive from other individuals.

I recall an incident I once had in my office. Following a return to school meeting which involved a student and parent, the parent involved had brought in a push chair which contained a small child. The meeting had gone well and the previously offending student had returned to class. On guiding the parent out of the building I engaged in conversation, passing the time of day, and asked about her other child who was residing in said push chair. The parent leaned over the quiet and smiling young one and with a huge grin on her face and caring, nurturing expression she said something I will never forget. In a warm and friendly tone, she uttered 'You're a F***in' little Bastard, aren't you?'
In response to this the child smiled and gurgled reading the extremely positive body language and facial expressions that their mother was giving them.

This summed up, for me, how much importance is put on non-verbal communication and also how children can be given mixed messages about the appropriateness of language used. This young child will grow up thinking that language used by their parent in that situation is a positive and therefore nothing wrong with using offensive language.

Body Language:

Facial Expressions:

'The Look'. Each and every teacher has a 'Look'. This normally consists of a raised eyebrow or a frown which suggests to the recipient that they are not pleasing you with their current choice in behaviour. I would highly recommend practising your 'Look' in the mirror in order to get the correct look for any particular situation. Although this may sound ridiculous you would be surprised as too how much you can achieve with a well timed, well chosen 'Look'. My wife, who was Behaviour Manager within a PRU, once suggested to me that she would like Botox treatment which would remove the frown lines she had between her well coiffured eyebrows. My response was text book, with my head tilted on one side I retorted 'Those lines make you, you. The laughter lines give you character and aside from all this you would not be able to do your job'. Following the puzzled look on her face I explained that an emotional less, blank expression would not enable students to understand what you want from them. This also saved me several hundred pounds!! Bonus!

Gestures:

Non-verbal cues are extremely important for teachers in keeping the flow of the lesson without interruption. There are a number of non-verbal cues that you should or will be already aware of.
- The 'Pen Down'
- The 'Mobile Phone in pocket'
- The 'Hood down' or 'Hat off'
- The 'Head phones out'

All these gestures and more allow you to continue teaching whilst dealing with the low-level behaviour, at a low level.

Tactical Positioning:

One of my favourites and well used tactics.
I first became aware of this tactic when I was actually at school. We had a Design Technology teacher who will remain nameless, who had perfected this technique. Although we were in a Design Technology classroom with a variety of tools and materials we never touched any of them and instead we were tasked with essays every session. These

essays had to be completed in silence and therefore, inevitably one of the unfortunates known as, my classmate, quietly tilted his head towards the nearest participant to ask a fairly innocuous question, such as, 'What you doing tonight?' This resulted in a world of pain and anguish as Mr X seemed always to be behind the student who had broken the rule of silence. I am sure that Mr X walked silently, as if imitating Nosferatu, and had a sixth sense for who was going to be his next victim.

I use the word victim wisely as Mr X was a member of the Territorial Army and therefore classed as a weekend warrior. The next method of discipline must never be used in this day and age as it will result in immediate disciplinary action with unemployment pending. Going back in time over 30 years meant that Mr X was able to get away with it.

Once the un-silent victim had been identified and locked onto, Mr X appeared behind them quickly prodding the pressure point behind the ear lobe. This caused severe pain, particularly due to the surprise attack. This resulted in the unsuspecting victim throwing their head back and normally uttering an obscenity. At this point Mr X had already thrown his arm back, cocked and ready for the well timed slap to the back of the head shouting 'and that's for swearing!!' as contact was made.

You are probably wondering why this story is being told, this was my first experience of tactical positioning.

Mr X, possibly unwittingly, was the master of tactical positioning. He taught most of his lessons from the back of the classroom so that we were unaware of which direction he would attack from and did not know where he was at any point during the lesson where as Mr X on the other hand was able to observe the entire class and position himself in the areas that needed more surveillance, while ensuring his presence was felt where and when necessary.

This is exactly what is meant by tactical positioning.

Positioning yourself where you are able to see the majority of the class, the majority of the time means you are aware of everything that is going on in your classroom and this in turn allows you to pick up on the low level behaviour before it escalates. This is most important when helping individuals. Do not bend over them, but instead 'take a knee' allowing surveillance of the rest of your students whilst aiding the individual.

Proximity:

Throughout all the above tactics, always be aware of your proximity to the individual you are dealing with. The younger the student, the less likely they are to understand 'personal space'. A very easy way to explain this is by holding your arm out in front of you.

Everything from the fingertips outwards is called 'Social space'. This is space that you are happy for anybody to enter. From the fingertips to the elbow represents 'Personal space'. This is space that you are happy for friends to enter, however, you may feel uncomfortable for others to cross into. The final distance which is from the elbow to your torso is known as 'Intimate space' or, as I prefer, 'Invitation only space'. As its name suggests this is the space that only very close companions are allowed to inhabit for short periods of time.

I have found that even the youngest of students are able to identify with this and aside from keeping your personal space free of youngsters it also enables them to understand how they should interact socially, without causing any unnecessary unease.

Although proximity with students is important to keep in mind there maybe times that you as the responsible adult have to make contact with the students in order to prevent injury to themselves or others. In order to safeguard yourself it is important to understand how to approach the individuals safely. During any training I deliver with regard to this I role play the 'Lift Exercise'.

Imagine you are in a lift and after stopping at the next floor someone enters the lift and stands directly in front of you in your personal space, uncomfortable! At the next floor this person exits the lift, however, just as your tension reduces another person enters the lift and stands directly behind you in close proximity, even more uncomfortable! At the next stop, to your relief, this person leaves and another takes their place, however, they stand next to you. Even though this individual is touching your upper arm with theirs it feels more normal and comfortable. This can be seen on public transport every day. Whilst on a bus or train people regularly stand in close proximity, side on to one another. Even though this is the only time within the lift exercise someone actually touches you this feels the most comfortable. For this reason, I will always, wherever possible, approach a young person from the side. This is less threatening than barrelling in from the front and also less surprising than approaching them from the rear.

Verbal:

Clear and Precise instructions: (Keep it simple!):

This is another one of my all-time bug bears. The number of lessons that I have observed where the teacher stands at the front of the class and delivers a long stream of instructions before letting the students loose on an exercise.

e.g.
'We are working from the Blue books today, page 12, exercise 5, question 1 through to 5 and 9 through to 11. Go!'
This inevitably results in a large number of students unable to remember the set of instructions which will immediately result in chattering amongst themselves while, between them, they are trying to workout what they are actually meant to be doing. The same teacher will often follow this with a phrase, such as, 'There is too much noise in here, what's all the talking about. You should be getting on with the task by now!'

Keep instructions simple, clear and broken down into small tasks. For the visual learners also write it down and for the Kinaesthetic learners show them what they should be doing!

Take up time:

For those of you that are not familiar with the phrase 'take up time' this is vital.
When faced with a student who is failing to complete work, any number of teachers may approach and ask why they are not or have not completed the task in hand. The first mistake is that they asked a 'Why' question (never ask a Why question, I will come to that soon!) and the second is that they will often stand over said student expecting them to crack on with the task immediately. When this almost certainly fails to take place, the member of staff in question will regularly stand over the student and continue to berate them for not doing it then and there. This is called 'Pecking someones head' and I have yet to see a positive outcome from such a tactic. Imagine your line manager asking you to complete a task and after agreeing to complete the task they continue to stand over you and ask you why you are not doing it now. After a number of these repeated requests, I guess, you will eventually be brought to boiling point when you will kindly ask your line manager to leave you alone for a wee while. As you are a professional adult this polite request would be expected, however, the same cannot always be expected from a student who is possibly feeling stressed as they are struggling with the task and almost certainly unable to express this request in such eloquent terms.
Take up time allows you to ask the participant if they need some support, direct them to the task if they have suggested they do not need the support and walk away. This gives them time to digest the instruction and then make the choice as to whether they complete the task. After giving positive feedback to a number of students who are following the instructions well (positive role modelling) make sure you keep an eye on

the young person who is failing to carry out the task. After approaching a second time and repeating the same offer of support and task instruction walk away once more.

If the student makes the choice not to be on task following the second interaction the language of choice should be used in order to put the onus on the student and the responsibility of the outcome on their decision.

Language of Choice:

This is incredibly powerful. I believe that all behaviour is a choice and that 90+% of students know right from wrong and also make an informed choice on how they behave.

It is for this reason that they should be held responsible for those choices and have to live with the consequences of their actions.

As human beings we make choices every second of the day and as a result of these choices we receive either positive or negative consequences dependant on the choices we make.

I often ask the question 'Why do most people, do the right thing, the majority of the time?' Answer: Fear of negative consequences!

We see people regularly speeding due to the fact that in the big scheme of things it is unlikely you will get caught as long as you keep your eyes peeled for Police officers and cameras etc., however, when some body is caught speeding they will inevitably spend the next few weeks obeying the speed limit. This is because it now registers higher within their consciousness and the risk that it is possible to get caught.

What the 'Language of Choice' does is offer the perpetrator a choice of consequence.

e.g.

'If you continue to behave in that negative manner, you are choosing a 'negative consequence', if you choose to complete the task then you will receive a 'positive consequence'.

A statement like this puts the accountability firmly back in the hands of the young person. By giving them the choice, they would be hard pushed to argue with the decision they made. It also abstains you from any negative consequences put in place as it was their decision, not yours.

In one of the centres that I managed, the 'Language of Choice' was so embedded by the staff that the students actually started finishing our sentences. As they also knew that the staff were consistent and would carry out the consequences, both negative and positive, some of the most difficult students began to self-regulate as everyone would prefer a reward over a punishment.

Never ask the students a 'WHY' question:

This is possibly the easiest of all the tactics and yet also the most difficult. From an early age we are encouraged to ask 'Why' questions.
e.g
- Why is the sky blue?
- Why is the grass green?
- Why do we need to eat? Etc.

As a result, it is programmed into us to ask 'Why' questions, which is why it is so difficult to give these up. Even after delivering this message to thousands of Teachers over the years through training, I still find myself occasionally asking a 'WHY' question before kicking myself.

The reason that you should never ask a 'WHY' question is simple when it comes to behaviour. 'You never really want to know the answer'.

Q:'Why did you throw that at Timmy?'
A:'Cause he's a dickhead!'

Q:'Why did you punch Timmy?
A:'Cause he deserves it!'

Q:'Why are you not completing the task?'
A:'Because it is shit and boring!'

None of these answers were what you were either hoping for or probably expecting, however, we continue to ask these 'WHY' questions. Judgmental, assumption of guilt etc.

What I propose is to not ask 'WHY?' but more 'What just happened?' This allows the student to tell you their side of the story without the assumption of guilt or just seeing one side of the story.

Positive reframing statements:

'Don't think of a white Elephant!' We have all heard this on any number of occasions, and yet, every time we hear this statement I can almost guarantee that we still think of a white elephant even though we are told not to.

The reason behind this is that the brain is programmed to take in information in a designated process. Therefore, we hear 'Think of a White Elephant' and then process the 'don't' bit.

As teachers who are constantly giving instructions, it is important that we take this into consideration and tell the young people in our care what we would like them to do, rather than what we would not like them to do, positively framing the instructions we give.

Statement	Positive alternative
Don't run!	Walk, thank you
Don't swear!	Please use appropriate language, thank you
Don't speak to me like that!	Speak to me politely as I do to you, thank you
You shouldn't be in here!	You need to be outside now (or) Where should you be?
What do you think you are doing?	Please put that away and get started on the task, thank you
Stop wandering round the room and get on with your work!	Back in your seat, thank you
I'll deal with you later	I'd like to sort this out now but the class are waiting; we will talk after school.
Stop pushing into the queue	Wait your turn in the queue, thanks

The use of 'Thank you':

Aside from being the polite thing to do. I tend to finish all my instructions with 'Thank you' as many of you will understand this infers that they have already decided to comply with the instruction. This is a bit of a Jedi mind trick but it does work. You will be amazed at how often you can use this in order to get what you want.

Para-verbal:

Para-verbal is the phrase given to, not what we say but how we say it. As stated earlier in this chapter most communication happens through body language and the cues we receive, and not actually the content of our spoken word.

Para-verbal focuses on Tone, Volume and Cadence.

Tone:

Assertive not aggressive! I have been asked on a number of occasions 'What's the difference and how can you tell if you have crossed the line from Assertive to Aggressive?' NLP have a phrase 'The meaning of your communication is the response you get.' This sums up exactly how you tell the difference between the two. If you get a cowering or aggressive response from your clientele you have crossed the line into aggression. I also see aggression as a sign of losing control rather than an assertive approach which signifies being in control.

There are an obvious number of reasons why you shouldn't stray into the realms of aggression, however, one of the main reasons for this is that you may be entering the students comfort zone and realm of expertise.

If you consider what the home lives of some of your clientele maybe you will no doubt have some students who arrive at school from very dysfunctional families. These young people will often be very used to communication which involves shouting, screaming and possibly violence. They are, hopefully, far more used to these environments than you and as a result will be in their comfort zone and far more practiced at dealing with and responding to this sort of behaviour. If you step into their realms of expertise be ready to lose. The other way to look at the reasons for not stepping across the line is part of our job is to teach them that there are different ways of responding to issues and getting a positive outcome.

Volume:

An increase in volume is OK as long as you are in control. The difference between a raised volume and SHOUTING is easy to identify.

In my opinion shouting happens when there is a loss of control and is often teamed with a face that resembles the colour of a Ribena berry and a totally involuntary wagging finger.

Being able to continue with the lesson as though nothing has happened is a key identifier that you have just increased your volume and are still in control. A need for a strong sweet cup of tea and a lie down following an altercation means you have simply lost it and instead of a controlled, raised volume you have entered the realms of a shout!!

An increase in volume is acceptable, and in some cases, required in order to assert your need for better behaviour from individuals or groups. As long as you are in complete control this will allow you to be heard and emphasise the importance of what is being said.

Cadence:

Cadence is always the one that people are unaware of and possibly the most important of the three. Cadence is the 'Rhythm and Rhyme' of speech.
I always remember a fact-based programme which proved that if people read statements in the form of a poem, more people would agree with the statement.
To be absolutely clear, I am not suggesting that you should teach all your sessions in the form of poetry, however think about the sentence structures of a poem. It is the inflexions within the speech and the fact that it is not written in a monotonous way.
The rhythm and rhyme of speech in a non-monotone voice is what keeps people interested and more likely to listen and retain the information offered. As educationalists we have all sat through lectures taught by individuals who would not be able to find a personality if it bit them on the backside and who impart knowledge in a way which is basically giving facts in a monotone voice. How many of us have been at the point of sleep within a very short period of time or through frustration and boredom have been driven to conversations with others next to you or mischievousness just to keep you from drifting off. As professional adults we should be able to maintain concentration. If we can't, faced with a boring monotonous lecture, how do we expect teenagers or the like to keep on task.

Chapter Six:
GRADUATED RESPONSE

As mentioned elsewhere in this book, a response that equally matches the intensity of the incident is extremely important. Dealing with low level incidents at a low level creates an atmosphere of fairness and also gives you, as the professional, a lot more directions to go depending on the students response to you.

A 'Graduated Response' to behaviour allows you to move up the continuum in a slow and controlled manner using a variety of techniques, strategies etc. before arriving at the consequences if and when necessary.

Below is a 'Graduated Response Continuum' which was formulated back in the 1970's by a fabulous behaviour specialist name of Bill Rogers. This sums up the number of different phrases and strategies that can be used before resorting to the negative consequences from the least intrusive to the most.

My recommendation to you is, that if you take nothing else away from this text, make sure you read the continuum below and digest it. This will stand you in good stead and allow you to reach into the tool box you have as a professional and bring out the phrases that are highlighted and put them to good use.

'GRADUATED RESPONSE CONTINUUM'

F.U.F.T
F.U.F.T – Follow up and Follow Through even though Senior Leaders maybe involved
COSEQUENCE 4 – Parents consulted
Poor choice again – Pupil sent to appropriate / identified leader
CONSEQUENCE 3
Third formal reminder – A poor choice again will mean a subject teacher resolution meeting – Detained at some point
CONSEQUENCE 2
Second formal reminder – Tick against name – Make a GOOD CHOICE
CONSEQUENCE 1
First formal reminder – Name on board – Make a GOOD CHOICE, Follow instructions

BLOCKING
"Work over there, thanks" – repeat and repeat.....and repeat!!

IMPLEMENTING CONSEQUENCE
"Jo – your choice, you've chosen to talk loudly – work over there now thanks

SIMPLE CHOICE
"Work quietly here, or you will be choosing to work over there"
"in your bag or on my desk thanks"

PARTIAL AGREEMENT
"Maybe – but" then "<u>maybe</u> you think it is boring<u>, but</u> .. it's a link chain – interesting bit next

TACTICAL PAUSING
Pause .... In mid-sentence – scan the class – wait for eye contact/take up time –
"Full attention thanks"

USE AN 'I' STATEMENT INSTEAD OF A 'YOU'
"Jack – I need you to look this way thanks" "Jill – I find that language offensive"

ASK A 'WHAT' QUESTION
"What should you be doing?" – repeat and repeat, (ignoring secondary behaviour) –
never ask a "why" question!!

CLASS ROUTINES / RESPONSIBILITIES
"Jack – what's the routine for entering the classroom?"

CLASS RULES
Ask about the rule –
"Jack – what's the out of seat rule?" "Jill – the agreed rule is follow instructions first time, thanks"

SIMPLE DIRECTION
"Jack – finish the map you're working on thanks" "Jill – the instruction is work quietly, thanks"

B.O.D.O.R
"Bleedin' Obvious Description Of Reality" – "There's a lot of noise in this room and not everyone has their books out yet!"

TACTICAL POSITIONING
Wandering nonchalantly over to the "hot spot" – just to be there!!

NON-VERBAL CUEING
Eye contact, raised eyebrow - knowing smile – raised hand, (open palm) – finger to lips – posture, change of stance etc.

TACTICAL IGNORING
Ignoring low level and 'secondary' behaviour – attending to on-task behaviour when pupils isn't making a bid for attention

The confident teacher/leader using positive correction – managing "Behaviour for Learning" from the head, not the gut!!

Chapter Seven:
Consequences

As mentioned throughout this book, 'Most people do the right thing most of the time, due to fear of negative consequences!' Although consequences should not be your only tool in your arsenal negative consequences do have a place when used correctly and within the framework of rules and regulations that you work within.

First and foremost, you must know the school policy and consequence system better than your clientele. The students that sit in front of you on a daily basis will be well versed in the school's system (particularly the young people who receive the most consequences ie. The naughty boys and girls). If you are unaware of the school's policy on sanctions, such as, The Traffic Light System, C1, C2, C3 etc. then do become aware quickly so that you are confident in the use of it if it becomes necessary.

This is also very true of the rewards system, know it well and in depth, use this liberally!

Avoid racing through the system:

During my time within the classrooms of others, I can safely say that this could be the most abused of all the rules.

One lesson observation I took part in saw a student removed from the lesson within a three-minute period from the start of the lesson. This went something like this:

Staff member was late to lesson. Students had already entered the classroom and a group of students were misbehaving.

On entering the classroom the member of staff picked the student I should have been observing and whilst pointing in his direction uttered the phrase 'C1'.

As there were a number of other young people carrying out similar behaviours the student in question remarked on how unfair this seemed.

The member of staff retorted 'C2 for answering back'

Undeterred at this injustice the student suggested that this was 'Bang out of order!'

The member of staff using the school's consequence system to full affect shouted 'C3, get out!'

Now although the staff member had followed the school's policy to the letter, I personally don't believe that their actions were fair and the teacher obviously wanted the identified student to be out of their lesson as quickly as possible. The student was later removed by the Senior Leadership Team (SLT) and the teacher was later given some extremely harsh feedback from me with regard to the way they handled the situation.

This clearly outlines what is meant by racing through the consequence system. The school's policy is there to aid but if you race through it very quickly and to the letter it is likely you will have an empty classroom on occasions and also have nowhere to go with the students aside from handing over to the Senior Leadership Team (SLT) which although it sorts the problem in the immediate time frame doesn't do any good long term. I will visit this later in this chapter.

Another common mistake I have seen being made on any number of occasions is the threatening of a consequence that is not within the power of the member of staff. As the only member of a school team who is able to Fixed Term Exclude a student is the Headteacher, staff who threaten young people with a Fixed Term Exclusion within a session are walking on very thin ice and are undermining themselves. By issuing such a threat and then not being able to carry it out is giving the young person every excuse in the world to treat you with a level of disrespect you may never have experienced before.

When discussing the use of consequences, it is important to remember that the consequence applied must always, not only be in proportion with the crime committed but also be individualised and fit the situation. There are students that you will or have come across when in education that want to be sent out of the class, as mentioned previously, this fulfils a number of roles, not limited to, but including, the fact that they do not have to complete the work and also this can be the start of a game of hide and seek with the Senior Leadership Team whilst perhaps meeting up with friends at a predetermined time and place. For obvious reasons sending these particular individuals out of a session for misbehaviour can actually be seen as a reward. On the flip side there are some students who would be absolutely mortified by the fact that they may be seen stood on a corridor outside a classroom. It is for these reasons each consequence should be considered carefully and dished out appropriately depending on the individual, environment and time of day. It is about knowing your clientele and what the most appropriate negative and positive consequences are to have the desired effect. In terms of the punishment should fit the crime, having a plan and a big choice of options that you can quickly and effectively put in place will instill further confidence when actually applying the sanction. Something to remember is manage your state successfully, this will allow you to put the most suitable and thought-out sanction in place.

Please also pay attention to the triggers and antecedents of the behaviours you feel necessary to punish, as it is often the case that staff will react to the behaviour they see / hear rather than the actual situation. This in turn means that often the behaviour we are punishing are that of the retaliator rather than the instigator. Always try to see the bigger picture and by investigating the causes of the behaviour will allow you to make more informed decisions and also build a reputation for being firm but fair.

In relation to delivering appropriate consequence it is imperative to understand that the certainty and immediacy of a sanction is more important than the severity of the sanction. What I mean by this is, a number of educational establishments use a centralised detention system. This means that in these institutions there is a process where the students, when asked why they are in detention are unable to answer due to the length of time it has taken for the young person to get to the detention, sometimes through no fault of their own but due to the system that the establishment enforces. My personal view on this is, what is the point of a punishment that the punished doesn't know what they are being punished for. It is therefore my view that the teacher must do everything in their power to ensure the student in question can understand what they have done wrong and also how to rectify the situation in the future. This can be done at break times, after lesson (in transition), lunch times etc. As soon as you can possibly put the consequence in place! The other element of the above statement is the certainty of the consequence. Although this is hard work it will pay dividends in the long run. By being like a 'dog with a bone' when it comes to tracking students down and making sure they fulfil the sanction that has been put in place will ensure that students are less likely to try and avoid and also if they are aware that you will ensure they complete the sanction they are unlikely to try and earn a negative consequence from you in the future.

Don't undermine yourself with the use of SLT:

When starting out in education a large number of NQT / RQTs will regularly look to their Head of Department or Senior Leadership Team to support them with their classroom behaviour management. Unfortunately, by relying on their support, visiting the classroom etc. actually undermines the NQT. By SLT arriving to sort out or remove a problem from the classroom they are sending out the subliminal message to the young people that the member of staff who is teaching them is not able to deal with their behaviour and they have to get help. This in effect is destroying your reputation for being able to deal with behaviour. Now this does not mean that you should not call for help where you feel it is necessary, however, if and when this does occur it is imperative that you follow this incident up by a conversation with the student who has been dealt with by SLT. By visiting the offending student as soon as possible after the incident gives you an opportunity to explain that you chose to, rather than needed to, involve SLT at that point as you had a group of students who were ready to learn and that your focus needed to be with them. This also re-establishes the fact that you are not scared of confronting the issue and are happy to deal with the individual at a more suitable time.

Remember: Consequences are often seen as negative, however, every choice we make in life has consequences and these are often positive. Do not forget to give positive consequences (Rewards) regularly.

Catch them being good!!

Chapter Eight:
What makes a good teacher – The young people have spoken!

Over the years that I have been working in the education sector, I have often asked the young people I have worked with, what they feel make a good teacher.

Following these informal discussions with students I compared the young people's views that I had collected with some research that had been conducted nationally. The results were remarkably similar and can be summed up very succinctly, below:

- Smiles
- Smartly dressed
- Eye contact
- Strong tone of voice
- Humorous
- Prepared – Work already on the board
- Shares safe personal information
- Deals with and follows up on issues promptly
- Is expressive
- Doesn't look nervous
- Moves around the class

I don't feel there is anything on the list above that is out of the ordinary, and therefore, we, as educationalists, should be able to commit to making sure we tick most of the above, metaphorical, boxes each and every day we step in front of our audiences.

If you are not ticking the boxes or not willing to move towards ticking the boxes you need to ask yourself why.

Conclusion

If you have got this far I trust you have enjoyed the read and you have gained something, however small, from it.

I am aware that pro-active and effective behaviour management is not as complicated as brain surgery and also aware that the majority of this is based on 'Common Sense', although my father has often said 'Common sense isn't common anymore!'

I hope in times of crisis in the classroom that you may reflect on some of the topics / chapters covered in this manuscript and that it may jog your memory as to what to do next.

In summary please find below my closing Top Ten Tips for positive behaviour management.

1. Get to know your students
   - Who is at home?
   - What are their interests / hobbies?
   - What are their strengths and areas for development?
2. Meet and Greet at the start of every lesson
3. Positively acknowledge your students on the corridor
   - Smile
   - Praise correct uniform
   - Praise and reward positive and appropriate behaviour
4. Catch them being 'Good'
5. Try and incorporate different learning styles into each lesson (VAK)
6. Tactically position yourself in the classroom to divert and avoid low level behaviour
7. Be aware of 'What you say and how you say it!'
   - Tone, Volume and Cadence
   - Assertive not aggressive
8. Use a graduated response when dealing with any level of behaviour
9. The certainty and immediacy of a sanction is more important than the severity
10. Ensure any sanction is in proportion to the situation and the individual

Thank you for taking the time to buy and read this book.

Take care

THE END

Printed in Great Britain
by Amazon